GREAT WARRIORS

GLADIATORS

KATE RIGGS

CREATIVE ✦ EDUCATION

Published by Creative Education
P.O. Box 227, Mankato, Minnesota 56002
Creative Education is an imprint of The Creative Company
www.thecreativecompany.us

Design and production by Stephanie Blumenthal
Art direction by Rita Marshall
Printed by Corporate Graphics in the United States of America

Photographs by Alamy (Ian M. Butterfield, Lordprice Collection, Mary Evans Picture Library,
Robert Harding World Imagery), Corbis (Alinari Archives, The Art Archive, Bettmann, Christie's Images,
Stapleton Collection), iStockphoto

Library of Congress Cataloging-in-Publication Data
Riggs, Kate.
Gladiators / by Kate Riggs.
p. cm. — (Great warriors)
Summary: A simple introduction to the Roman warriors known as gladiators, including their
history, lifestyle, weapons, and how they remain a part of today's culture through sports such as wrestling.
Includes index.
ISBN 978-1-60818-000-4
1. Gladiators—Rome—History—Juvenile literature. I. Title. II. Series.
GV35.R54 2011
796.80937—dc22   2009048804
CPSIA: 040110 PO1137
First Edition
2 4 6 8 9 7 5 3 1

TABLE OF CONTENTS

Sometimes people fight.

They fight for food. They fight for land.

Or sometimes they fight for sport.

Gladiators were warriors who fought

other people to **entertain** crowds.

Many gladiators became very famous warriors

Gladiators began fighting more than 2,000 years ago. They lived in lands that belonged to the **Roman Empire**. Roman soldiers captured slaves, **criminals**, and other men. They forced these men to become gladiators. Sometimes people **volunteered** to be gladiators, too.

Gladiators sometimes had to fight beasts instead of men

SOME **EMPERORS** FOUGHT AS GLADIATORS. THE
EMPEROR COMMODUS LOVED FIGHTING IN THE **ARENA**.

7

Gladiators were sent to special training schools. They learned how to fight with swords and other weapons. They learned how to defend themselves. And they learned everything they could about how to win a fight.

Some gladiators used nets, spears, and clubs

Gladiators fought in arenas. Most gladiators used a shield and a sword. The swords were usually short and sharp. Some gladiators used nets or spears in a fight.

People in Rome liked to watch gladiator fights

THE MOST FAMOUS ARENA IN THE CITY OF ROME WAS
THE COLOSSEUM (*KAH-LUH-SEE-UM*).

Fighters could not wear much clothing to protect themselves. But most gladiators wore helmets. Some wore leg or arm guards made of leather, too.

Leather is a material made from animal skin

Gladiator battles did not last long. When a gladiator was too hurt to keep fighting, he fell to the ground. The emperor decided what happened to the loser. He decided if the loser would live or die.

Gladiators fought one or more people at a time

WHEN THE EMPEROR GAVE A THUMBS DOWN, THAT MEANT THE LOSING GLADIATOR GOT TO LIVE.

SOMETIMES GLADIATORS
FOUGHT AGAINST
BIG, WILD
ANIMALS LIKE LIONS
AND TIGERS.

When gladiators were not fighting, they trained for the next fight. Some gladiators married and had children. Most gladiators had to live at their training school.

Lions and tigers came to Rome from faraway places

A slave named Spartacus trained to be a gladiator. But he ran away. He led thousands of other slaves in a fight against the Roman army. A famous gladiator named Spiculus was rewarded for being a good fighter. The emperor gave him land and houses.

Spartacus died on the battlefield more than 2,000 years ago

Some emperors did not want people to kill each other for sport. They tried to stop gladiator fights. But gladiators kept fighting until the early 400s A.D. Today, boxers and wrestlers fight for sport, but not to kill. Gladiators live on in them!

Gladiators sometimes fought with their hands like boxers

GOOD GLADIATORS WHO WON A LOT OF BATTLES COULD STOP FIGHTING AND LIVE TO AN OLD AGE.

GREAT WARRIORS HAVE LIVED ALL OVER THE WORLD. THIS MAP SHOWS WHERE SOME GREAT WARRIORS LIVED. GLADIATORS WERE IN ROME. KNIGHTS WERE IN EUROPE. SAMURAI WERE IN JAPAN. PIRATES SAILED ON THE OCEANS.

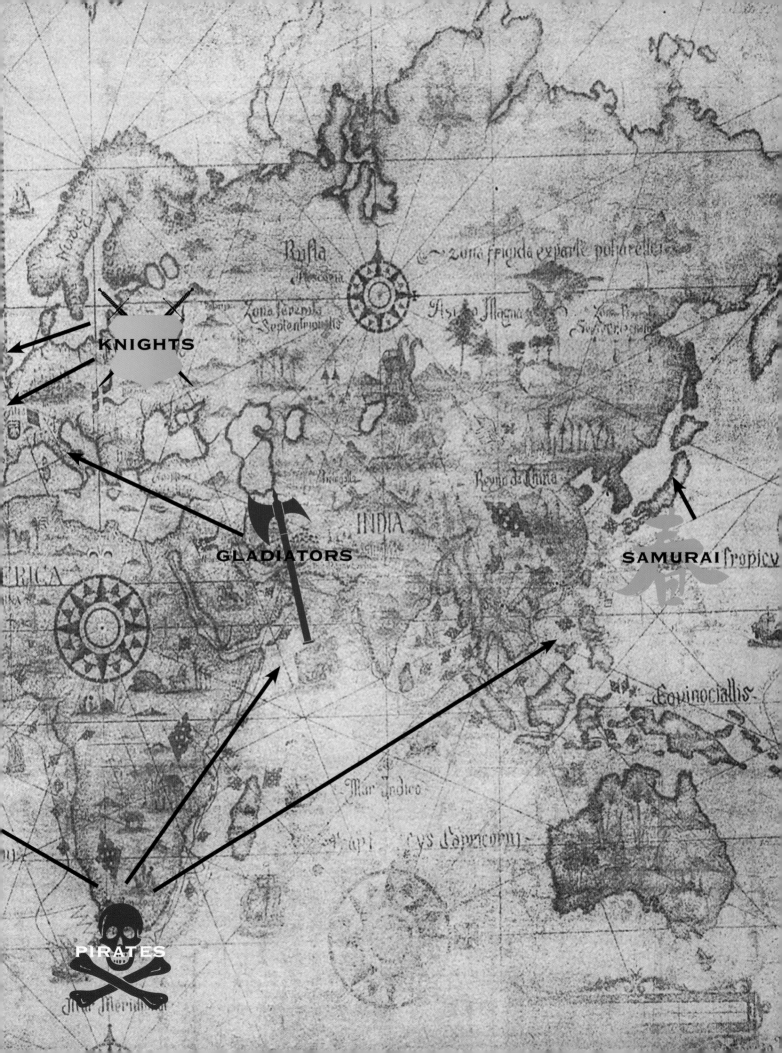

GLOSSARY

arena—a large, flat area for fighting that was surrounded by many seats

criminals—people who break the law

emperors—powerful rulers who control their kingdoms, which are called empires

entertain—to make people laugh, cheer, or pay close attention

Roman Empire—all the lands and people controlled by the ruler of Rome, a city in Italy

volunteered—did something without being forced into it

READ MORE

Ganeri, Anita. *Gladiators and Ancient Rome.* Milwaukee: Gareth Stevens Publishing, 2005.

Martin, Michael. *Gladiators.* Mankato, Minn.: Capstone Press, 2007.

INDEX